# Transformational Leadership with Humility and Grace

# Vicki Escudé

An Executive Coach shares an "inner path" to becoming a truly great, transformational leader!

Transformational Leadership

is not what you "think."

# Reviews for *Transformational Leadership with Humility and Grace*

In a world riddled with uncertainty leaders bear the responsibility of visioning with minimum sight, confronting fear with no certainty of success and plunging into the future without clarity. This book pierces the problems to reveal the substance of how leaders can transcend these obstacles to uncover the essence of leadership. It shows the way beyond tradition. Every leader in today's world should be required to read this book. **Joan C. King, PhD, Master Certified Coach, Author of the Cellular Wisdom series of books and *A Life on Purpose: Wisdom at Work.***

*Step 1:* Take a 360° tour of yourself as a leader.

*Step 2:* Look in the mirror.

*Step 3:* Ask if you are seriously interested and ready to make the commitment to launch your leadership to the next level.

*Step 4:* Turn your back on the mirror because what you see is not really you, just a reflection of your outer self.

*Step 5:* Buy and move through this book that invites you to reveal your amazing inner self that holds the key to being a transformational leader. This book is hazardous to your status quo. Be prepared to warp drive into awareness of *who* you truly are. Reflections and contemplations about leadership philosophy, strategy, relationships, communication and culture abound for your journey.

*Step 6:* All you need to do is allow your wisdom to emerge. **Teri-E Belf, Master Certified Coach, Author of *Coaching with Spirit*, Global Director, Coach Trainer, Success Unlimited Network®**

Working with Vicki has helped me to become a more reflective, insightful, creative, and empathetic leader. In turn, my leadership efforts have resulted in meaningful and sustained outcomes. This book, *Transformational Leadership with Humility and Grace*, provides an easily implemented prescription for authentic and efficacious leadership. **Chuck Powell, CEO, Encompassing Leadership Associates, PhD Candidate, Leadership and Change, Antioch University**

**Attention:** For copies and information, contact Vicki
Escudé, Executive Leadership Coaching, LLC, at
Vicki@excellentcoach.com, or www.excellentcoach.com
Discounts available for quantities.

# Dedication

*To the bright spirits of Leon, Laura, and Chandler
– my inspiration!*

# Books by Vicki Escudé

*Getting Everything You Want and Going for More!* *Coaching for Mastery*

*Create Your Day with Intention!* *The 30-Day Power Coach* (in English, Portuguese and Spanish)

*The Philosophy and Practice of Coaching* - Contributing Author

*Fast-Track Leader: First, Master Yourself!*

*Revel in Your Wisdom – Kybalion Deck Booklet,* with Teri-E Belf

*USNA Life! Families, Homes and Treasured Memories of the United States Naval Academy*

# Table of Contents

# Introduction

Become an effective, inspiring leader from the core of your BE-ing. Leadership is a powerful vehicle for your personal and spiritual growth. Within *Transformational Leadership with Humility and Grace* are Reflections, Contemplations and poignant Questions that will transform your leadership philosophy, strategy, relationships, communication and organizational culture. Carry this handbook with you throughout your day and your travels for focus, serenity, and inspiration! In times of organizational and economic stress, it's the best gift for your soul's equilibrium and sense of peace.

We have been taught that good leaders become effective by honing their communication skills and demanding productivity. Masterful leadership that inspires transformation, however, is much more than skill development. It is a significant inner challenge, and you will know when and if you are ready to take it on. It will be a "calling," or a deep soul yearning.

Transformational leadership is about noticing those significant inner shifts, so that you become an effective, inspiring leader –inside and out. Who are you becoming as you increase your ability to lead? What is your daily discipline to keep you on track, your ego in check, and your values in focus? The process is less of "acquiring information and skills" and more of a "letting go" of what is getting in your way of expressing your authentic self.

Much is being written about "Transformational Leadership" as a cutting edge concept. However, it is as ancient as the human soul. Lao Tzu in the *Tao te Ching* from 2500 years ago understood this path.

To paraphrase verse 17 of the *Tao te Ching*, the leader who is a true Master is in the background. He is not the leader who is feared, despised, or even the one they love. He knows that to expect his people to be trustworthy, he must first trust them. He speaks very little and carefully takes action. When the Master-leader completes his work, the people all say, "*We* did it!"

The essence of Masterful Leadership from the description in the *Tao te Ching* is "humility." Humility and right action set the stage for the gift of grace. Thus, the focus of this book is on the elements of humility and grace to accompany personal transformation.

If you are ready for this step in leadership, ask yourself, "Am I willing to let go of 'force' and move into 'personal power?' Am I willing to have others say, 'We did it ourselves?'" If so, then your leadership role will become a mindful, spiritual practice. It will be that higher calling and a form of thoughtful discipline. The terms "self-actualizing," "transformational leadership," "coaching leadership" and "masterful leadership" can be used interchangeably to describe this approach.

How do you get from here to there – to be able to fully integrate the transformational leadership concepts into your daily actions? Well, it is a step-by-step process. Are you ready to step forward?

If you join me on this journey, together we will explore different aspects of personal and spiritual growth and leadership. How might you approach these topics in a way that hastens and deepens your own self-discovery?

*Transformational Leadership with Humility and Grace* involves increasing your inner awareness and changing old habits, patterns and attitudes. The ability to change patterns is enhanced by being open to fresh ideas, and fresh ideas nurture a new awareness of who you are and who you choose to be.

This book can be your feast for new ideas and your coach for personal and professional transformation. You will find tools for self-reflection, tools for action, tools for personal and professional growth, and a reminder to grow through humility.

A playful attitude is essential to leading with humility. Humor is life's very own means of keeping a perspective, of not taking yourself seriously. Enjoying your participation in the journey paves the way to attract what you want. The leadership topics of Philosophy, The Transformational Leader's Strategy, Transformational Relationships, Transformational Communication, and a Culture of Transformation are designed to support positive energy, insights and change. The most important thing you can bring to this playground is your enjoyment of the process.

Let this be your playground. Begin now! Imagine the joy of blazing a path for others to create a better world – inner and outer!

**The Feather Touch:**

Have you ever had something "fall in your lap" when you least expected it – good fortune smiled on you just after you let go of wanting it? This is "Attracting What You Want" in a nutshell. Instead of "working your heart out" to become an effective leader, wouldn't you like to have it show up in your life more easily, working "with heart?"

The secret is this: developing leadership behaviors is about "inner" work first. Rather than trying to make something happen, which brings up resistance and struggle, you can begin to attract results by *being* in a state of enjoyment. Notice that the "Be-ing" comes first.

That does not mean you can sit around and do nothing! You can, however, shift your focus, so that hard work is eliminated. Attraction does include the word "action." There are still action steps to be taken, but achieving through attraction means that the actions to be taken are more harmonious, thoughtful, efficient, and hopefully fun! Why use a sledgehammer when the light-feather touch will suffice?

## The Inner Work

By applying your "inner work" first, you are more at ease, quiet, confident, and able to feel or hear those gentle nudges from your Inner Guide or your intuition. The "inner work" helps you to remove obstacles, so you can see the path to your goals more clearly.

What is this "inner work?" Spending time each day contemplating one individual topic is your jump-start. You will be prompted to journal your thoughts for deeper contemplation, and for taking action. Setting your intentions based on who you choose to be that day, and also expressing gratitude comprise "inner work."

Most of us would rather roll our sleeves up and start moving ahead, doing, doing, doing, but laying a firm foundation with contemplative time is the key to shifting to a higher level of personal achievement and becoming the leader of your dreams.

## This book is for:

- Leaders.
- Executive Coaches and Consultants.
- Leaders who want effortless change.
- Leaders who care about leading with integrity and strength.
- Leaders who have a deep commitment to supporting others to grow and learn.
- Leaders who have a "higher calling."

- Leaders who see the value of leading with humility.
- Leaders who choose a path of transformation.
- Leaders who offer opportunities for others to transform.
- Leaders who embrace a "coaching style" of leadership.
- Organizations that aspire to creating a "Coaching Culture" or "Learning Culture."

# How to use the tools in this book:

Reflective time is productive time – a habit all transformational leaders must adopt. Discipline is important to create new patterns of thinking and pathways toward leadership. Are you committed to becoming a transformational leader? Will you commit to daily reflection? Is it worth the investment of your time and energy?

Set aside reflection time daily using "Reflection" questions, which invite you to personalize and actualize each leadership topic.

**Morning:**

Morning time, before you get out of bed, over your morning coffee, or when you first sit down at your desk are times when your awakening self is open and fresh.

Whatever you focus on at that time will influence your experiences for the day. Reading a new, inspiring idea and reflecting on how you truly want to BE that day gives you a head start toward successful daily experiences.

## Evening time or bedtime:

At the end of your work-day, as a part of your transition to the evening time and personal time, review the focus you have chosen for the day, and complete the evening gratitude process.

Or, bedtime is a time to unwind, reinforce new ideas, and reflect on positives for the day using the vehicle of "Gratitude."

In either case, the inner self will begin to look for and attract positive experiences during your daytime so that you can notice them in the evening. During this process, release any negative patterns and worry from the past and allow them to stop at that time, so that you will begin with a clean slate the following day.

Setting up positive expectations on a daily basis will help you develop new patterns for success. The individual tools within the leadership topics will help you to move powerfully forward to achieve the transformation that is meaningful and purposeful to you.

As you adopt new, positive leadership patterns, a new leader in you is born! You will begin to recognize and connect with your fellow-travelers as you move forward on your path of growth and transformation.

# Prologue

The leader leans back in his well-worn, familiar office chair, springs creaking like perennial companions, his weight against its constant support. And just like the springs, he feels worn and stretched, yet still vibrant, still viable.

Reflecting on his journey to this pinnacle in his career, he experiences the calm serenity and deep gratitude for the journey which has unveiled the mystery of all mysteries – who he really is.

This is what he sought all along, this jewel in the crown of leadership. The journey was not for accomplishment, aggrandizement, wealth or fame. It was simply a vehicle for self-mastery, to know his true nature, and to experience his connection to the All. Who would have ever known his work-day world would be replete with opportunities to connect with Spirit as well as daily clues as to where to place his foot next on the path?

Although he chose this singular, deeply personal way to grow, not needing guidance or accolades from others, he discovered that through his own development, others around him grew, as well. By simply accepting full responsibility for himself, he expected it of others. And, they obliged.

In searching for and honoring his own inner wisdom, he nurtured it in others. They called him the Transformational Leader. He never acknowledged that title. He was only a fellow-seeker, an humble partner with others in the life mastery process, playing his part as it was revealed to him, not as he might choose.

His "Inner Knower" hinted of a new level in this journey toward mastery. He had no idea what might be next, but he had learned well that to swing forward, like the courageous trapeze artist, one must first let go of the trapeze bar and fly for a moment unaided.

So, just at the moment he rises from the comfortable chair, heeding an inner urge to move on, a messenger comes to the door.

"Sir," said the messenger, "Your car is waiting for you to go Home."

# Part I

## The Philosophy

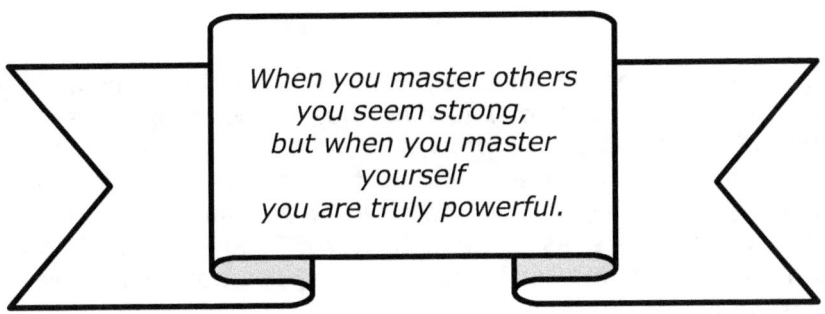

*When you master others
you seem strong,
but when you master
yourself
you are truly powerful.*

*Paraphrased from Verse 33 - *Tao Te Ching*. Written by Lao-tzu , 6th Century BC.

# The Transformational Leadership Shift

Leadership with humility and grace requires a new leadership paradigm. The leader does not rely on finely honed skills to be "great." Nor does the leader become "servant," which is the other end of the spectrum.

Leadership with humility and grace requires a shift in perspective. Leadership simply arises from the leader's *inner* orientation; it becomes an automatic outcome of a new relationship to self and life.

This transformed leader asks, *"Who do I need to become in order for leadership to naturally arise?" "What qualities in me will invite others to grow and develop their potential?" "How might I forge a path so that others will want to follow?" "How might I re-create who I am and allow others to take my place as I move forward?"* She notices how others are showing up in her life now, to support her own learning.

The humble leader, therefore, is focused on:
- Becoming self-actualized and self-aware.
- Inspiring others to grow to their potential by simply being on that path herself.
- Allowing others to teach her.
- Noticing who and what are prominent in her life now for her own learning purposes.
- Expecting others to replace her and take her role at each level of her own journey, thus creating space for new leaders to emerge.

---

**Contemplation:** *How might I begin to focus on my development as a transformational leader, and demonstrate the path for others to follow?*

---

# Reflection

*My challenges with the Transformational Leadership perspective are:*

_____
_____
_____
_____
_____
_____
_____
_____
_____
_____
_____

*The concepts and principles that support Transformational Leadership that attract me are:*

_____
_____
_____
_____
_____
_____
_____
_____
_____
_____
_____
_____

# Inviting Partnership

The transformational leader still "leads," but the transformational path gives the leader the opportunity to change the dynamics of the relationship with direct reports. There can now be a "partnership."

This partnership empowers employees to begin thinking for themselves, taking responsibility, and being inspired by their experience of growth.

How does this work? The leader must communicate to others that he fully trusts their wisdom and answers. When this attitude is established, the communication serves to support the employees' insights and development.

The leader's questions become respectful, out of sincere curiosity, and prompt employees to make their own discoveries. The leader also begins to listen deeply, looking for clues to help others unlock their potential, as well as clues for the next step in his personal growth.

Allowing an employee to make mistakes without retribution also supports growth. The partnership then becomes one in which both parties are able to explore together what worked and what did not work, so that the learning can be more impactful.

With this transformational approach, it is as if the leader and direct reports are walking respectfully together on a path toward awakening. They become partners in the journey.

---

**Contemplation:** *How might I invite transformational partnerships with others in my organization?*

---

# Reflection

*Ways that I still cling to the traditional approach to leadership in my organization:*

_____

_____

_____

_____

_____

_____

_____

_____

_____

*I move toward "partnership," and learn to communicate in ways that support the growth and wisdom of others by:*

_____

_____

_____

_____

_____

_____

_____

_____

_____

_____

_____

_____

# The Power of Humility

Humility and leadership seem opposites. Humility, however, comes from a place of power and strength. In the solid core of a leader are found the inner peace and stillness of an humble person.

What does it mean to embrace "humility" within leadership?

- Being humble comes from strength, not weakness. When a leader is humble, she does not have to prove herself. She is so secure and self-loving that she knows her own worth, and does not need it validated.
- The humble leader does not "self-promote." She carries her wisdom within, and her power comes from the accumulation of experiences. There is no need to draw others' attention to her achievements, as who she is at any moment reveals her growth.
- The humble leader is quiet, not intentionally attracting attention. She feels safe in every situation, and has no need to exert force over others out of fear.
- She is gentle and non-judgmental of others, because she sees the God within them, their true nature, and knows the pain and suffering within the desperation that most people carry.
- She listens and learns from situations, rather than giving directives based on limited information.
- She is centered and calm, serving as a strong anchor for others caught in the maelstrom of life.
- "Humble" has the following synonyms: modest and unpretentious.

---

**Contemplation:** *How might those whom I lead benefit from a leader who is humble? How might I, as a leader benefit?*

---

# Reflection

*My challenges to being humble as a leader are:*

_____

_____

_____

_____

_____

_____

_____

*Practicing the discipline of humility would strengthen me in the following ways:*

_____

_____

_____

_____

_____

_____

*I am noticing the benefits of humility in my daily life as:*

_____

_____

_____

_____

_____

_____

_____

*I see the difference between "humility" and "meekness" as:*

_____

_____

_____

_____

_____

_____

_____

# Right Alignment

In an organizational climate it might seem impossible to expect support on the Transformational Leadership path. How can one shift to this new perspective in a spiritual vacuum, which is often found in today's hierarchical leadership models and practices?

The answer is simple: The Transformational Leadership path is singular. One chooses the path, and follows one's own inner guidance. The relationship is to ones "Self." The Transformational Leader does not need support or advice from others to keep focused and to experience growth. Wisdom comes from within, and only your own counsel would work for you anyway!

In addition, this path is not one of competition, power, one-upmanship, or winning over others. If these goals or experiences are desired, another approach to leadership would be advised. There are plenty of role-models for other leadership categories.

The success of the Transformational Leader comes from increasing self-actualization, and any outward recognition from others springs from the growing inner strength, wisdom, and singular focus that has become a part of the leader's persona. In other words, recognition is not sought, but when it does come it is because of the sure and steady inner evolution of the Transformational Leader. Recognition is feedback, not the goal.

---

**Contemplation:** *How might I listen for and trust my own inner guidance?*

---

# Reflection

*When I am striving to be "on top" or to attain continual recognition, I experience the following:*

_____
_____
_____
_____
_____
_____
_____
_____
_____
_____
_____
_____

*Some strategies to shift from wanting to "be on top" to choosing "inner expansion and connection" might be:*

_____
_____
_____
_____
_____
_____
_____

*Values that support my personal and spiritual growth are:*

_____
_____
_____
_____
_____
_____
_____

# Why Humility?

Humility in a Transformational Leadership role is a strategy and discipline for growth, an attitude that will help remove roadblocks from the path. Humility must be used with a desire for learning - not manipulation. It is for the purpose of personal, intentional growth - not for feigning agreeability simply to gain compliance.

When you adopt humility as a discipline to support transformation, you are saying to yourself and reflecting to others:

- "I don't know the answers."

- "I am equal to you and respect you."

- "When my mind is clear or empty, I can hear my inner voice more clearly."

- "I am willing to learn from you and with you."

- "I suspend my negative judgments and opinions, remaining open to what you offer now."

- "No matter who you are, I salute the God in you from the God in me."

- "I am not separate, better or lesser, but am One with you."

- "You are a mirror for me to see myself more fully."

Staying on track with humility asks you to be fully present and be able to let go of the past. Humility, then, is an invitation to the spiritual experience of "Oneness."

---

**Contemplation:** *How might an attitude of humility help me to learn from others? How might I develop an open, clear, and "present-focused" mind?*

---

# Reflection

*When I approached a situation with humility, I learned the following about myself and the situation:*

_____

_____

_____

_____

_____

_____

_____

_____

_____

*Others whom I have observed as having an attitude of humility are:*

_____

_____

_____

_____

_____

_____

_____

_____

_____

*How might I more fully engage my "Inner Knower" to guide me in times of adversity or uncertainty?*

_____

_____

_____

_____

# Grace

Transformational Leadership calls you to be watchful for clues for learning and right action. An attitude of humility positions the leader to be alert for those clues and those moments of grace, which nurture the spirit.

Perhaps you can recall a time when you were struggling "upstream" against the current of life. At some point you realized that the struggle was overwhelming or even useless, and let-go or shifted your perception. By turning your gaze around to the other direction, "downstream," you began to flow with ease toward your greater good, with grace.

Grace is that state in which the leader has re-aligned with the natural flow in life, the situation surrounding her, or the people involved with her. It is as if life's current is moving toward peace, and the leader is, for the moment, flowing with joy in the state of grace. A new course is set, and she trusts the magic and miracle of the experience.

Grace is the leader's signpost that assures "all is well." It cannot be manipulated into being and there are no skills to set it in motion. It is an "allowing." Grace is an allusive state of being, and beyond words.

Grace is a gift. The transformational Leader recognizes it when it arrives, accepts it with an open, humble heart, and is deeply grateful.

---

**Contemplation:** *How might I look and listen for, and be open to the gift of grace in my life?*

---

# Reflection

*These days, my "upstream" struggling is in the following areas:*

_____

_____

_____

_____

_____

_____

_____

_____

*Times I have experienced grace in my life have been:*

_____

_____

_____

_____

_____

_____

*Ways I might shift my perception of my struggles, and begin the "downstream" flow, inviting grace, are:*

_____

_____

_____

_____

_____

_____

_____

_____

# Forward Focus

The term "Transformational Leader" might give you pause. You might think that you are too old, have a past that is too tainted, too unremarkable, or that it will take too much effort to move toward the greatness of personal mastery.

This path, however, is not about heroic effort. It is about letting go, and experiencing alignment with a natural flow. It is about "effortlessness," a concept that is difficult to embrace simply because it is not how we have learned to accomplish things.

What would it take for you to believe that:

- Your success will be measured by your experience of the incredible and courageous journey you choose?
- The earth will rise up to support you, reality is kind, and every event is for your positive growth?

When you let go of past expectations and begin to take one step at a time, the flow will begin, the support will become apparent, and at some point you will move forward effortlessly. Often, it's the first tiny step that makes the difference.

---

**Contemplation:** *Am I willing, just for today to choose to become a more mindful and humble leader, and take only one small step in that direction?*

# Reflection

*I hold myself back from becoming a Transformational Leader by:*

_____
_____
_____
_____
_____
_____

*One small step to move through my barrier is:*

_____
_____
_____
_____
_____

*New thoughts or beliefs to support my forward movement are:*

_____
_____
_____
_____
_____
_____
_____
_____
_____
_____

# Going Forward Gently!

We often groan when we think of "change." It sounds like a big, ugly, unwelcome, overwhelming struggle. We think of multitudes of small steps to be taken each day until the mountain has been climbed. Even thinking about change is tiring!

What works is to develop *supportive attitudes* toward your visions, dreams, intentions or results. Picture them, say them, and then let go of making them happen. Use a feather touch!

Imagine having them come to you "effortlessly," in a state of grace, while being surprised! Tell yourself every morning, "Today **I AM amazed** at how my personal, professional, and spiritual aspects are growing." Let the state of grace spill into your day easily, as you stay sharp for cues to take action.

And, express gratitude.

---

**Contemplation:** *What if I were amazed at how my vision and dreams are unfolding today?*

---

# Reflection

*Today I will support my Leadership Vision by:*

_____
_____
_____
_____
_____
_____
_____

*Today I noticed movement toward my Leadership Vision in these ways:*

_____
_____
_____
_____
_____
_____
_____
_____

Evening Reflection:

*I experienced a sense of Grace today in the following ways:*

_____
_____
_____
_____
_____
_____

# The Gift of Adversity

The actualizing leader learns to flow with adversity. Adversity shifts from being a problem to solve with your tool kit of acquired skills to an opportunity for learning, growth and transformation. Adversity has the potential to move the leader and the organization out of old paradigms into fresh perspectives and new directions.

Reframing adversity changes the energy of the involvement from one of resistance, negativity and struggle, to the positive energy of acceptance, curiosity and solution-focus.

Adversity, then, becomes the bell-ringer for positive change. What are the supportive actions and reactions to this signal of change?

- Lead with curiosity. Ask, "What is the opportunity here?"
- Lead with creativity. Ask, "What are possible creative responses?"
- Lead with vision. Ask, "What new vision might we create?"
- Lead with solution-focus. Ask, "What next steps take us meaningfully forward?"

Notice the lack of blame, looking backward, or holding onto the past. The Transformational Leader quickly embraces adversity, shifts the energy of the situation to positive, and leads forward with efficiency, effectiveness, and with an eye for learning and growth.

---

**Contemplation:** *What are fresh ways to interpret any adversity I am experiencing at present?*

# Reflection

*Ways that adversity is showing up for me and my organization now are:*

_____

_____

_____

_____

_____

_____

*My opportunity is:*

_____

_____

_____

_____

*Possible creative responses are:*

_____

_____

_____

_____

_____

*My new vision is:*

_____

_____

_____

_____

*Next steps forward are:*

_____

_____

_____

_____

# Embrace Change

Change is the only constant in this reality. The Transformational Leader embraces change because it heralds learning and growth.

If you have been taught to "use your mind" to succeed in your career or personal life, then think again. Your mind-set, or beliefs, may be keeping you stuck in age-old, outworn, self-defeating patterns, like Sleeping Beauty under a spell.

Logic might tell you to learn new tactics for a better career, or a better personal life. But these strategies fly out the window when you are faced with everyday stress and unanticipated obstacles. You find yourself reacting in the old, same ways because your patterns run too deep.

Old thought patterns and behavioral habits feel safe and comfortable, like a well-worn shoe. *Change* is fearful. Therefore, anything new is met with great resistance, and may not feel as safe. The Transformational Leader learns to stalk change – to seek it out rather than be blind-sided by the inevitable.

The Transformational Leader can break the imprisoning enchantment by examining old, limiting beliefs and by choosing new beliefs. New beliefs will support new behaviors and bring new opportunities to learn.

Identify your fearful thoughts – put them into words. Challenge yourself to find evidence that the negative beliefs are not true. Then, gently invite a new perspective that supports your goals, your dreams, and your success as a leader.

---

**Contemplation:** *How might I choose new beliefs and embrace the positive change that will unfold as I move toward leadership with humility and grace?*

---

# Reflection

*When faced with change, in the past my first reaction has been:*

_____

_____

_____

_____

_____

*The benefits of change in the past have been:*

_____

_____

_____

_____

_____

_____

*New perspectives that support embracing change are:*

_____

_____

_____

_____

_____

_____

_____

_____

_____

_____

_____

# Part II

# The Transformational Leader's Strategy

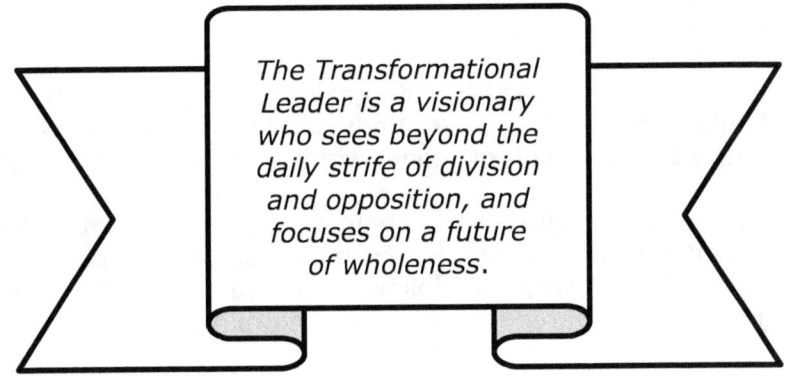

The Transformational Leader is a visionary who sees beyond the daily strife of division and opposition, and focuses on a future of wholeness.

# Be-ing before Do-ing

The Transformational Leader is aware of "being." She asks, "*Who* do I bring to my new day?" before she asks, "What do I do today?" When "being" is grounded and balanced, actions spring forth easily with a sense of grace, and are natural – never forced. Activities flow easily, like a dance. And, like a trained dancer who hones her skills behind the scenes, the transformational leader does the "inner" preparation necessary to outwardly demonstrate wisdom with humility.

To create this sense of grounded centeredness, the Transformational Leader finds discipline and rituals to support a new habit of "going within" before "going forth."

What are the rituals that help you become centered yet poised for action, like a martial artist who is still before moving? To what disciplines will you commit? Is your growth and awareness worth this commitment?

One suggestion is to reflect each morning on how you choose to "be" that day. What qualities do you wish to exhibit?

---

**Contemplation:** *How might I be intentional about my experiences daily?*

---

# Reflection

*A ritual or inspirational discipline to which I commit daily is:*

_____

_____

_____

_____

*The benefits of honoring this discipline are:*

_____

_____

_____

_____

_____

*Today I choose to reflect on the following qualities that give me a sense of well-being:*

_____

_____

_____

_____

_____

*At the end of the day, I noticed the following effects of my focus on well-being:*

_____

_____

_____

_____

# Gratitude: A Transformational Tool

Tucked away on the bottom of a page was a two-sentence article entitled: "On the bright side: counting blessings is healthful."

The article boldly states: *"New research shows that people who consciously remind themselves every day of the things they are grateful for show marked improvements in mental health and some aspects of physical health. The results appear to be equally true for healthy college students and people with incurable diseases, according to new research published in the Journal of Personality and Social Psychology."* *

There you have it!

**Leadership Challenge**: You may have heard about the power of a "Gratitude Journal." Here is a slightly different twist that produces great, significant changes in people's lives.

Every evening, before going to sleep, mentally identify and record 5 things that happened that pleased you that day.

---

**Contemplation:** *How might I be grateful daily, knowing that this is a powerful way to create well-being and be the thoughtful and aware leader I choose to be?*

---

*Savannah Morning News, 3/10/03*

---

# Reflection

*Ask yourself: How does a daily practice of gratitude support the concept of Leading with Humility?*

_____

_____

_____

_____

_____

_____

*Evening Reflection: Tonight I express gratitude for what worked, what supported me today, or what pleased me:*

_____

_____

_____

_____

_____

*My gratitude helps me learn and grow each day in the following ways:*

_____

_____

_____

_____

_____

_____

_____

_____

_____

_____

_____

_____

# Connect with your Highest Values

Once you adopt a spiritual path using leadership as your vehicle, you may find your personal values have shifted. The importance of "recognition and acknowledgment" may be replaced with greater emphasis on "integrity," for example. Check into your values, so you may use them as lamps to illuminate your inner journey.

Tapping into your values and aligning them with your dreams gives your visions more meaning. A values-based life is a passionate life – just the juice you need to support your authentic self. Do you know your personal values?

**Actions:**

*Step #1:* List five leaders you admire – from any era! What are their top qualities? Are they things like endurance, fun, patience, enthusiasm, integrity, honesty, humility – or a myriad of other values? List these qualities beside their names. Look for common themes, and choose qualities that have meaning for you.

*Step #2:* The qualities you admire in these leaders are also your higher values, because what you see in others reflects what is meaningful to you. List your top "values."

Step #3: Take the top qualities that are your highest values, and reflect on what you already express, and also on what you would like to develop. How can you demonstrate these values daily in your life? Create a "Values Statement." When you do, you will be in touch with your authentic, passionate being.

> **Contemplation:** *How might I joyfully demonstrate my core values daily in my personal and professional life, creating a life of meaningful passion and authenticity?*

# Reflection

*My higher values from the exercise are:*

_____

_____

_____

_____

_____

_____

_____

_____

_____

_____

*My values statement is this:*

*I demonstrate the higher values of* _____,
_____, _____, _____, *and* _____ *in*
*my life and work daily.*

*Today, I demonstrate my higher values in the following*
*ways:*

_____

_____

_____

_____

_____

_____

_____

_____

_____

_____

# The Twins - Dreams and Fears

There is an excitement and thrill that comes with your journey to becoming an awakened leader. However, hiding in the shadow of your dream is its twin, fear.

Most people do not get beyond the fear. They feel or think that something is wrong with their higher vision. They would much rather give up their dreams and goals than look at the fear. This resistance is natural, and an important survival function of the mind.

The mind equates surviving with status quo, staying the same. "Stay the same," it whispers in your ear. "You won't survive if you try something new." Thank your mind for doing its job and helping you survive, then reassure it that you can change AND survive.

Spend some meditative or quiet time brainstorming possible stretches for yourself. A hint is to look at what you might have some fear around doing. The fear may be a clever cover-up for your passion or your next big step. Write down your next small step toward a "stretch" goal. Then, take another look at your fear. How does it feel now?

---

**Contemplation:** *What greater awareness or opportunity to expand is my fear hiding? What is on the other side of the fear that is a gift?*

---

# Reflection

*My leadership vision and my personal/professional growth bring up the following fears or hesitation:*

_____
_____
_____
_____
_____
_____
_____
_____
_____
_____

*When I experience fear, being stuck, or any hesitation today, my strategy will be to:*

_____
_____
_____
_____
_____
_____
_____
_____
_____
_____
_____
_____

# Rekindle Your Passion

As a Transformational Leader you will inspire others because you are inspired by your vision and values. However, when your well is dry, others cannot take nourishment from you. Being on "automatic pilot" daily with no time for rejuvenation diminishes your sense of aliveness and dampens your passion.

Take time to let loose of old structures and routines. Sit by the pool or on the beach, watch an inspiring video, take a course in something that intrigues you. Allow yourself to be nourished in creative and fun ways. Perhaps a spiritual retreat or time for personal renewal can rekindle and expand your connection to the Inner Voice. Maintaining your sense of well-being and balance will keep your inner spark glowing, and serve as inspiration to others.

**Take action:** Break old patterns. Brainstorm some creative and fun ways to keep fresh and inspired, and choose to take action on them.

Have some FUN!

---

**Contemplation:** *How might I tap into my passion today by creating new, inspiring patterns in my life to find ways to awaken my aliveness?*

---

# Reflection

*To support new patterns and creativity, I can refresh my passion and be inspired today and in the future by:*

_____

_____

_____

_____

_____

_____

_____

_____

_____

_____

_____

_____

_____

_____

_____

# Staying Present

Staying focused on the present moment keeps a leader fresh, agile, and response-able. What throws the Transformational Leader off the path? Harboring judgments, opinions and limiting beliefs can shift one's focus away from learning and responding in the "now."

Judgments, opinions and limiting beliefs are based on decisions one has made in the past, and they inform how one will respond in the future unless they are examined. This attitude is like a hardened shell around a fresh oyster pearl. Old judgments lead to arrogance – the opposite of humility.

The path of humility requires the leader to continually notice set beliefs and suspend them. Unwrapping and unwinding beliefs is the "work." How can you spot an old, limiting belief? Look for any negative emotion – fear, sadness, anger. Look for set opinions of self and others – or "shoulds." Be mindful of "absolute thinking" – the idea that something or someone is *always* or *never* a certain way.

Staying present is adopting the "beginner's mind" and continually checking with your "Inner Knower." Be willing to see each person in the organization and in your life as new and fully capable in each present moment. Accept each new situation as a gift, a fresh opportunity for growth and greater awareness.

---

**Contemplation:** *Who might I become as I suspend limiting beliefs, and see each person and situation anew – in the present?*

---

# Reflection

*Opinions and judgments I have of people in my organization are:*

_____

_____

_____

_____

_____

_____

_____

_____

*What is some evidence that those opinions are not true?*

_____

_____

_____

_____

_____

_____

*How might I and others benefit from approaching each person and situation "in the present?"*

_____

_____

_____

_____

*Activities or people who support my being fully present are:*

_____

_____

_____

_____

_____

_____

# Create a Transforming Vision

Spend a few quiet moments either thinking about or visualizing how you would like your life to be different three to six months from now. As a Transformational Leader, who have you become in that time frame? What shifts have you made in your beliefs, perceptions, attitudes, discipline and practice that support transformation? What changes have occurred in your communication and relationships to support your personal and professional transformation?

Write your vision as a script, as if you are writing a scene in play in which you are the star! Make your vision sound "juicy" and compelling by adding "feeling" words, so that it looks and feels like you have already achieved what you want.

For example: *"I am happily sitting in my office, looking over my "to-do" list for the day, and notice that I am communicating effectively. My teams are highly productive and harmonious. I have re-defined how I see and experience leadership, which is . . . . My new outlook contributes to this success because I am practicing. . . . . I look forward to . . . . "*

Write down your vision and your script and read it daily for 30 days. Expect and notice the magic of transformation!

---

**Contemplation:** *How might I create a leadership vision that reflects the aware, self-actualized person I choose to become?*

---

# Reflection

*My Transformational Leadership Vision is:*

_____
_____
_____
_____
_____
_____
_____
_____
_____
_____
_____
_____
_____
_____
_____
_____
_____

*On a scale of 1-10, with 10 being highest, I am committed to this vision at the rate of _____.*

*If my rating is less than 10, the following would make my commitment a 10:*

_____
_____
_____

*This vision is a reflection of my priorities and core values in the following ways:*

_____
_____
_____
_____
_____

_____

# Humility and Grace 360 Degrees

Integrating the quality of humility and inviting grace into every area of life supports true, deep, and authentic shifts. When you bring them to all your life experiences, not just leadership, your ability to grow in your awareness multiplies. You can apply growth principles 360 degrees in your life.

Imagine how intertwined the different components of your life are. Your health affects your ability to lead. Your personal relationships impact your work-life balance. Your finances influence your ability to have fun.

What opportunities for growth would you have if you practiced humility at home with family, or with friends? How might transformational principles affect your relationship to your finances, or even your leisure time?

As you consider your ideal expression of each area, reflect on how you might apply humility and grace:

> Appearance/Health
> Career/Money
> Fun/Leisure
> Personal/Spiritual Development
> Home-Work Environment
> Relationships

---

**Contemplation:** *How does my Transformational Leadership path impact all areas of my life?*

---

# Reflection

*Specific ways that the practice of humility and grace might enhance my experience in different life areas are:*

*Name of Life area* _____:

_____

_____

*Name of Life Area* _____:

_____

_____

*Name of Life Area:* _____:

_____

_____

*Name of Life Area:* _____:

_____

_____

*Name of Life Area:* _____:

_____

_____

*Name of Life Area:* _____:

_____

_____

# Being 100% Responsible

We hear that it is the ex-spouse, the kids, the boss, our parents, the weather or the economy that has created havoc in our lives. The truth is that you are totally responsible for your success and effectiveness as a leader, and your personal and spiritual growth as an individual.

Your success is fully in your hands – always! The great leader faces all adversity with humility, knowing that each situation is a golden opportunity to grow. Accepting that he drew each situation to himself for a higher purpose helps to accept 100% responsibility. Understanding the purpose and power of all adversity helps keep the leader alert for learning and keen for expansion.

What would your life look like if you took full responsibility for your life and your success?

---

**Contemplation:** *How might I take full responsibility for my life, my work, and for the success and well-being I choose?*

# Reflection

*Ways I diminish my responsibility by blaming other people and situations are:*

_____

_____

_____

_____

_____

_____

_____

*Ways I can demonstrate full responsibility for my success today are:*

_____

_____

_____

_____

_____

_____

# Leadership Presence

Just as leadership with humility and grace requires a shift in perspective, so does the traditional view of Leadership Presence. One is taught that one's appearance, stance, and the ability to communicate in specific, well-schooled ways can produce or support effective leadership.

Instead, imagine that leadership comes from within you; the way you dress, stand and communicate are simple outward manifestations of who you are.

What attitudes create Transformational Leadership presence? These attitudes track with how you approach your life and your leadership roles. An actualizing leader:

- Is motivated from within, based on personal values.
- Is a learner, assessing each situation for growth and development.
- Displays emotional intelligence, springing from greater self-awareness and from thoughtfully choosing his responses.
- Is respectful of others' ability to grow and change.

A leader with this inner compass knows what is appropriate for each situation. How might your presence reflect your values, your willingness to learn, your thoughtful responses, and your inherent respect for others?

Leadership Presence with humility and grace requires diligence – a constant mindfulness of who you are in relation to current situations and to those around you. "Presence" is akin to being "present."

---

**Contemplation:** *How might I develop new attitudes toward Leadership Presence, to be more congruent with my path toward personal and professional transformation?*

---

# Reflection

*Opportunities to have greater Leadership Presence are available in the following areas:*

- *Demonstrating my values:*

  _____

  _____

  _____

  _____

- *Being a "learner:"*

  _____

  _____

  _____

  _____

- *Thoughtfully choosing responses:*

  _____

  _____

  _____

  _____

- *Respecting others' abilities and points of view:*

  _____

  _____

  _____

  _____

*Obstacles to demonstrating Leadership Presence are:*

_____

_____

_____

*Ways to overcome these obstacles are:*

_____

_____

_____

_____

# Discipline

The path to Leadership with Humility and Grace calls for developing a discipline, just as any spiritual path. Committing to discipline, even if it changes over time, is both grounding when you feel lost, or helps to raise you out of the mire when you are stuck.

What kind of discipline would benefit your leadership path? You might look to your "Allies." What helps them keep focused on higher values or spiritual principles? What have you experienced that connects you to Source?

Here are some disciplines to explore:

- Prayer
- Meditation
- Yoga
- Walking/running/physical movement
- Being mindful of thoughts
- Being mindful of words and language
- Exploring limiting beliefs
- Being of service with anonymity
- Journaling for self-awareness
- Reading inspirational writings
- Attending retreats to nourish body, mind and spirit
- Connecting with a wise "listener" – a mentor or a coach.

Using your intuition, what discipline for focus and higher connection resonates with you at this time?

---

**Contemplation:** *How might I choose ways to support my path, creating positive habits that carry me through times of doubt or stress?*

---

# Reflection

*Ways that I have experienced support in the past that help me connect with my Higher Self, and that keep me focused:*

_____

_____

_____

_____

_____

_____

*Some disciplines I choose to explore are:*

_____

_____

_____

_____

_____

_____

_____

_____

*Today I choose the following way or ways to support my path:*

_____

_____

_____

_____

_____

_____

_____

_____

# Draw from Strengths

Think of a time when you felt inspired as a leader. It could be a job well done, a goal achieved, or a personal realization. Think of ways you have contributed to work, family, friends, community, religious organizations, civic organizations, or life in general.

List what **strengths** you exhibited during these endeavors or during your moments of inspiration. Note your top strengths. Do you see any patterns among them? These are the qualities you offer to life, and to the achievement of your goals.

How can you use your strengths to support your Transformational Leadership path? How can focusing on your strengths increase your belief in your own inner guidance and wisdom? Acknowledging your positive qualities helps you to know you have an abundant well of strengths from which to draw. Drink deeply!

---

**Contemplation:** *How might I acknowledge and draw from my strengths, drink deeply from them, and joyously offer them to the world?*

---

# Reflection

*Times that I experienced my own inspired leadership are:*

_____
_____
_____
_____
_____
_____
_____
_____
_____
_____
_____
_____

*Strengths I used:*

_____
_____
_____
_____
_____
_____
_____
_____
_____
_____

# Maintain Balance

An humble, insightful leader is centered and balanced. Work/life balance occurs when you feel nurtured in all areas of life. Ask yourself:

How can I nurture myself every day?

- Do I want to meditate, pray or reflect every morning?
- Will I honor my health with exercise and sensible nutrition?
- Will I invest in my well-being by spending my first waking moments listing on paper how I choose to "BE" that day?
- Will I ask others to assist?
- What is NOT necessary for my health, well-being and enjoyment of today? What can I eliminate from my to-do list?

Taking care of yourself FIRST is not selfish! It is necessary, so that you will have enough to give. When you are filled – or self-fulfilled, it automatically spills over to serve others in a natural, flowing way.

In your leadership position, being a role model for balance and well-being yields results. Others will be inspired to emulate your lifestyle and attitudes. Inspiring others to be balanced helps them to stay fresh, creative and more productive.

---

**Contemplation:** *What healthy thoughts and actions might I choose today? How might I inspire a sense of well-being and balance in others?*

---

# Reflection

*The following are ways I can nurture myself, and support my personal sense of balance.*

_____

_____

_____

_____

_____

_____

_____

_____

*In what ways will I nurture myself today?*

_____

_____

_____

_____

_____

*If I prioritized my activities, what could I let go of?*

_____

_____

_____

_____

_____

# Mindfulness and Emotional Intelligence

A leader must demonstrate emotional intelligence, become aware of blind-spots, and learn how to shift emotions to avoid "knee-jerk" reactions. How can you change or re-pattern your negative thoughts, feelings and expectations?

One suggestion is that you create a "Notebook to Shift My Perspectives." Here's how:

1. List some problematic issues or people.
2. List everything that is positive or beneficial about these situations or people, creating one page for each topic or person. Make each list as extensive as you can.
3. Then, to create the new patterns, allow yourself to focus on these benefits. Read these positive pages daily.

What we are really talking about is replacing old thoughts and feelings with new ones. Two thoughts cannot exist in the same place at the same time. It is to your benefit to choose the thought that supports your well-being, and helps you to "feel good." It takes practice! Like shoes, pick thoughts that take you forward – toward that new, high stepping, well-tread YOU!

---

**Contemplation:** *How might I shift my thoughts and feelings, knowing that the return on my investment is growth and self-awareness?*

---

# Reflection

*As a leader, my most problematic situation or person is:*

_____

_____

_____

_____

_____

_____

_____

_____

_____

*Some positives about that individual or those situations are:*

_____

_____

_____

_____

_____

_____

_____

_____

_____

_____

_____

_____

_____

_____

_____

# Letting Go

When we want our lives to evolve, it is never about adding "more" of anything.  It involves, instead, letting go.

When you let go, you are participating in a miracle.  A miracle, according to *A Course in Miracles*, is not something that occurs without your participation.  It is not magic and not the "deus ex machina" of the ancient Greek plays that drops in to save the day.  A miracle is a shift or change in perception.  When you experience a shift in perception, your world also changes. It is your "light-bulb" moment.

What do you let go to create space for the new? You let go of limiting beliefs, attitudes, clutter, activities, habits, and even some friends.  Ask yourself:  "What no longer expresses who I truly am?"

Because this is a spiritual journey, the "letting go" process is akin to "surrender," to trusting your inner guidance.  It is like stepping onto an escalator and being moved upward to a new level of life, with ease. The outcome is a shift in perception – thus, the miracle.  The shift propels you to new action.

Before the new you is firmly in place, there may be an experience of emptiness or stillness. Enjoy this space, as you are creating a vacuum so there is room to attract something new.  It is like that brief pause between the in-breath and the out-breath. Remember to breathe deeply!

---

**Contemplation:** *When I choose to move to a new level of awareness, what am I letting go?*

---

# Reflection

*A new level of awareness for me is:*

_____
_____
_____
_____
_____
_____
_____
_____
_____
_____

*To live more fully within this level of awareness, I am aware of the following shifts in my activities:*

_____
_____
_____
_____
_____
_____
_____
_____

*To support my new level of awareness, I choose to take action, letting go of or re-evaluating my relationship to the following people, activities and material things in my life:*

_____
_____
_____
_____
_____
_____
_____
_____
_____

# Part III

# Transformational Relationships

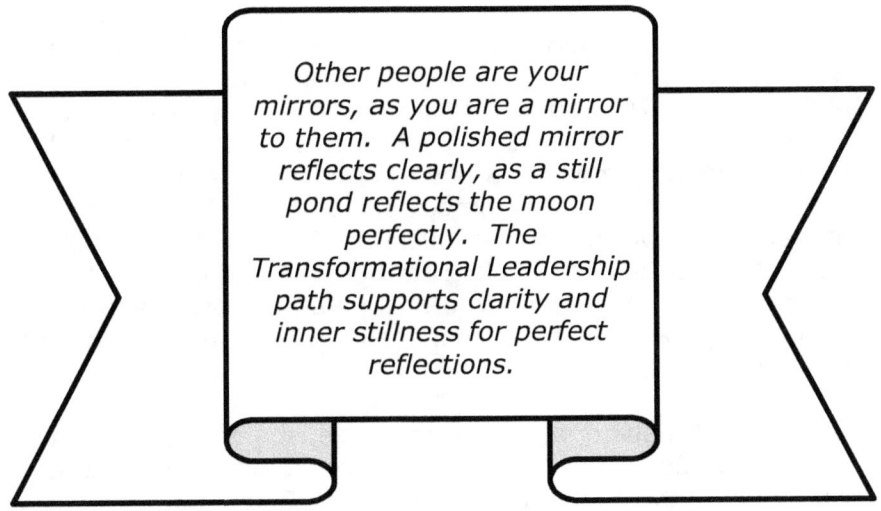

*Other people are your mirrors, as you are a mirror to them. A polished mirror reflects clearly, as a still pond reflects the moon perfectly. The Transformational Leadership path supports clarity and inner stillness for perfect reflections.*

# Choose your Allies

Because Leadership with Humility and Grace is a path, not a skill, you may no longer find value looking to contemporary business leaders and popular writings for guidance. However, finding allies and guides to support you will help give your path substance and keep you focused on your journey.

Who might these guides be?  They may shift from time to time.  You may be drawn to certain teachings or spiritual philosophies.  Ask yourself, "Who inspires me these days to connect with a higher Self or Principle?"  It could be a trusted friend or mentor, a philosopher, or a spiritual figure – a Jesus, Buddha, Mohammed, or Lao Tzu.  It could be a modern-day spiritual writer such as Eckhart Tolle, Byron Katie, Manuel Ruiz, the Dalai Lama or Esther Hicks.  Finding "allies" that resonate with you at a given time can help you aspire to greater heights, and their vision can serve as a beacon when times are cloudy.

One characteristic of an ally is someone who prompts you to rely on yourself – your own inner voice.  Gaining connection with Self is the ultimate connection to Guidance.  You no longer look to others for answers, but know that within the situation, the answer is inherent.  You become your own best ally, listening for inner counsel.

Your special and personal allies can become an invisible, internal "Board of Directors" for your unique and highly personal Transformational Leadership journey.

---

**Contemplation:**  *Who might I choose as "allies" to walk with me on my path?*

---

# Reflection

*Inspirational Allies for me are:*

_____

_____

_____

_____

_____

_____

_____

*My Allies can support my Leadership with Humility and Grace in the following ways:*

_____

_____

_____

_____

_____

_____

_____

_____

_____

_____

# Acceptance and Forgiveness

The path to enlightened leadership is sprinkled with opportunities to embrace and heal those parts of yourself you have denied.  Denial of your wholeness happens like this:  you see attributes in others that you judge as bad or wrong, yet you pretend these qualities do not exist in you. What you judge in others represents a part of you that you do not want to own.   This denial process is called "projection" because you project onto others what you cannot or will not see in yourself.

Are you willing to accept that the person or situation you judged negatively represents some aspect of you that needs reclaiming?  Is it possible that you have exhibited the same behaviors you judged in others?

You can move toward wholeness with the spiritual practice of "acceptance and forgiveness" of yourself and others.  The great leader learns to look within and embrace his lost bits. In truth, the other people or situations you judge are really your teachers; they are your perfect mirrors!

Self-forgiveness and acceptance of self and others lead to humility. You can forgive, reclaim those lost parts, and be grateful for the opportunity to grow toward wholeness.  A great leader courageously loves herself – warts and all!

---

**Contemplation:**  *How might I notice what I judge in others, accept those parts of myself I am denying, and move toward wholeness?*

# Reflection

*People or situations I have judged are:*

_____

_____

_____

_____

_____

_____

*What is more clear to me about those aspects of others and situations I have judged is:*

_____

_____

_____

_____

_____

*I choose to begin the process of forgiveness with the following people and situations:*

_____

_____

_____

_____

_____

_____

_____

# Values-Based Relationships

Alignment with values motivates you toward excellence. Values give meaning to your actions. A leader knows that those around them have the same internal compass in relationship to their own values.

Begin noticing what those around you value. How can you tell? Carefully listen to what they talk about or what activities they engage in. Is it their family, adventures, volunteerism, spirituality, or creative projects? Do they love to learn? Are they committed to their growth personally and professionally? Keep notes on what is important to others.

Being curious and respectful of others' values is a key to humility. It is humbling to take into account and appreciate what is important to others. Relating to others in terms of their values demonstrates respect. This respect can help forge a positive bond and relationship that will support productivity, harmony and willingness to be team players.

One step further is to connect values with work projects. How might the project support or connect with the expression of someone's love of family, sense of adventure, helping others, or growing and learning, or whatever they value most?

---

**Contemplation:** *How might I notice what other people value, show my interest in and respect for those values, and help them express their values at work?*

---

# Reflection

*I notice others' values:*

_____

_____

_____

_____

_____


*I can support their values in these ways:*

*Name_____:*
*Support:_____*

_____

_____


*Name_____:*
*Support:_____*

_____

_____


*Name_____:*
*Support:_____*

_____

_____


*Name_____:*
*Support:_____*

_____

_____


*Name_____:*
*Support:_____*

_____

_____

_____

# Expect 100% Responsibility from Others!

Interestingly, when you take full responsibility for your own success, you begin to expect others to take responsibility, as well. Take a quick survey of your work-day. What have you taken on that really belongs to someone else?

Leaders often take over what others should be doing because they are in charge, they often have the most experience, they think they can do the work more efficiently or effectively, or they want other people to "like" them. None of these are good leadership decisions for taking on more than your share. Doing so eats into your productivity and creativity – not to mention the havoc it brings to your time management.

When you expect others to do their job and take full responsibility, you are empowering them. They begin to grow, feel more competent and also take "ownership" of their work situation. They can begin to solve problems in ways that make sense to them.

The empowerment of others does not diminish your leadership. Instead, it gives you greater room for the development of your leadership path, and allows you time to cultivate more creative solutions and positive relationships – and to be the inspired leader!

---

**Contemplation:** *How might I choose to respect and empower others to be fully responsible for their lives and work?*

# Reflection

*Tasks that belong to others at work and at home are:*

_____

_____

_____

_____

_____

_____

_____

*Today, I assign responsibility to where it belongs, in the following ways:*

_____

_____

_____

_____

_____

_____

_____

_____

_____

# Relationships Will Change

As leadership with humility and grace requires stepping onto a new path – one of growth and spiritual alignment – relationships inevitably shift, as well. Relationships become mirrors so the leader can "see" himself more clearly.

Noticing how others are reacting, or by requesting feedback, the leader develops clues about what he projects. Are his values clear, judging from others' responses? Are his limiting beliefs and judgments tarnishing relationships? What is the general mood or tenor of the team or the organization, and how does your leadership presence influence that?

The actualizing leader also recognizes that leadership is a responsibility, and leaders must accept that their role is unique. He may find that the dynamics of old relationships begin to shift, and old buddies become more distant.

The Transformational Leader understands that people become prominent in their lives and then recede from view, depending on the learning and growing that the relationship offers. Thus, friends and colleagues take on a different role. They are vital players in our personal and spiritual development, and they may move on when the lesson is learned or the support is given. Knowing that the shifts he experiences are purposeful, the transformational leader can let go of attachment to the inevitable "coming and going" of friends and colleagues.

---

**Contemplation:** *Who is in my sphere these days that supports my growth and higher purpose? Who might I let go of at this time?*

---

# Reflection

*Reflect on and describe your current relationships with:*

- *Direct Reports*

  _____

  _____

  _____

  _____

- *Peers*

  _____

  _____

  _____

  _____

- *Superiors*

  _____

  _____

  _____

  _____

*Among my Direct Reports, Peers, and Superiors, what do my relationships reflect back to me these days?*

_____

_____

_____

_____

_____

_____

_____

_____

_____

_____

_____

# Building Positive Relationships and Support

Effective leaders build positive relationships - with humility and grace. In addition to being mirrors, relationships are also wonderful ways to maintain balance in your life. People can support you on your path, and enhance your awareness in your personal or professional life, or both! Using a car analogy, who in your life keeps your engine purring?

*Engine Diagnosis* - Ask yourself who provides the following types of support:

- Honest Feedback
- Acknowledgment
- Positive Energy
- Leadership Development

Now that your car is up on the rack, look at the above support categories. Ask yourself:
1. Which of the above categories have good support?
2. Which are lacking in support?
3. Do I rely on one or two people for support in many different categories?

Do your relationships need a tune-up? What actions will you take on your insights from the above questions?

> **Contemplation:** *How might I create and accept positive relationships in my personal life and my professional life today?*

# Reflection

*The following people support me with:*

- *Honest Feedback:*
  _____
  _____
  _____

- *Acknowledgment:*
  _____
  _____
  _____

- *Positive Energy:*
  _____
  _____
  _____

- *Leadership Development:*
  _____
  _____
  _____

*Ways I can develop support in the following areas are:*

_____
_____
_____
_____
_____
_____
_____
_____
_____
_____

# Get Out of the Way!

You may have heard the expression, "Lead, follow, or get out of the way!" Leadership with humility and grace proposes that you shift that paradigm, and think differently. How about, "Lead BY getting out of the way!"

The effective leader is described in Verse 17 of the *Tao te Ching* from 2500 years ago as one who works in the background, and lets others say, "We did it!"

This ancient wisdom is supported by modern-day educational researcher, Sugata Mitra with his inspiring "Hole in the Wall" experiment. Mitra, who was awarded the 2013 TED Prize, found that students can learn *on their own*, and *teach each other* despite dire and impoverished circumstances.

Imagine the growth and learning that people in your organization can enjoy given the considerable resources available to them! How might you demonstrate your trust by allowing them greater leeway to learn, grow and produce results with minimal direction and structure? Their creativity and ownership may surprise you!

Are you game? Are you willing to empower the people in your organization so they can say, "We did it ourselves"?

> **Contemplation:** *How might I let go of the traditional leadership-by-authority thinking, and empower others to use their own creativity and strengths to get our desired results?*

# Reflection

*I hold onto a traditional leadership model when I:*

_____

_____

_____

_____

_____

_____

_____

_____

_____

*Steps I will take to empower people in the organization to foster their creativity as well as their productivity are:*

_____

_____

_____

_____

_____

_____

_____

_____

_____

# Part IV

## Transformational Communication

Transformational Leadership gives one the opportunity to transform relationships and inspire growth through conscious communication. A lighthearted perspective, inviting partnership, and listening deeply are transformative for the leader as well as others around him.

# Lead with Light-heartedness

Developing light-heartedness is essential for your own balance and well-being, but also the well-being or those you lead. A "light heart" implies that:

- You are not unduly burdened by your own issues. You maintain a perspective by being mindfully introspective, seeing personal and professional road-blocks as stepping stones to greater awareness.

- You offer those you lead a perspective. When others' malaise or organizational issues are approached with a light heart, you invite them to trust that positive outcomes are possible.

What contributes to your lightheartedness and having an inner buoyancy? It might be your connection to the Divine – whatever that is for you. It could be that you truly trust your inner guidance to support your best interests in the long run.

Understanding that the Universe, Reality, Life are ultimately kind and good allows one to step back from problems, take a deep breath, and smile!

How would you rate your level of lightheartedness, these days? (1-10) _____.

---

**Contemplation:** *What shifts in my thinking will contribute to leading with lightheartedness?*

---

# Reflection

*Ways I can lead with lightheartedness today are:*

_____

_____

_____

_____

_____

_____

_____

_____

_____

*What I choose to believe, or my perspective on life that contributes to my lightheartedness is:*

_____

_____

_____

_____

_____

_____

_____

_____

_____

_____

_____

_____

_____

# Transformational Feedback

Whether it is for performance, annual reviews, development plans or daily requests, leaders have an opportunity to deliver feedback in ways that support growth and transformation in others. Giving feedback can either be a roadblock that creates resistance and ill-will, or an art that inspires people to action and personal growth.

Stepping back before delivering feedback is essential. Ask yourself:

- Is this the best time? What is the emotional climate?
- How might I prepare and center myself for the conversation to be most effective?
- How can I arrange for privacy to enable open and honest communication?

Consider the metaphor of a glass of water. If someone's "glass is full" of anxious or defensive thoughts, there is no room for feedback. In a transformational coaching way, it is prudent to help "empty his glass" first.

How might this look? First, be curious about your employee's perspective. What is his evaluation of the situation? Ask permission to share your observations. Acknowledge his triumphs and give honest, to-the-heart feedback. Then, together brainstorm ways new action might be taken. Inquire about any learning and positive results from the conversation. Discuss the opportunity for growth, as if it is a gift to him.

Through thoughtful feedback, leaders can contribute to the positive transformation of others daily.

> **Contemplation:** *I give feedback in a way that inspires others to action and offers the gift of transformation.*

# Reflection

*Obstacles to giving effective feedback have been:*

_____

_____

_____

_____

_____

_____

_____


*Steps I can take today to begin practicing giving effective, empowering feedback are:*

_____

_____

_____

_____

_____

_____

_____

_____

# Transformational Listening

The most important communication skill to enhance Transformational Leadership is "transformational listening." Being an active listener involves more than just hearing the other person's words, and responding.

Transformational listening involves the whole person – both the "talker" and the "listener." When someone is talking, are you fully engaged? When listening with full attention, you will intuitively notice what the person's body language and tone of voice is telling you. Are there any patterns in what the person is saying – are you able to "connect the dots" with past communications that will give you more information?

Good listening is like being on a treasure hunt. When you gather many clues, you will know how to express yourself in ways that the other person "hears" you.

Deeply listening lets others know you care about them and their point of view. When they feel deeply "heard," they are more engaged, more trusting, and are likely to listen to you when you speak. When what someone says "resonates" within you, and you have suspended judgment, they are given the opportunity for healing and transformation.

Stopping to deeply listen seems time consuming, however, it saves time in the long run. When others feel that they have communicated their thoughts and feelings to you and that you "got it," they can move on.

Contemplation: *How might I listen deeply to empower others, help them feel "heard," and increase my ability to communicate constructively?*

# Reflection

*My obstacles to being a "Transformational Listener" are:*

_____

_____

_____

_____

_____

_____

_____

_____

*Today I will take the time to listen in the following ways, and in the following situations:*

_____

_____

_____

_____

_____

_____

_____

_____

*The results I experienced from "Transformational Listening" today are:*

_____

_____

_____

_____

_____

_____

_____

# Transformational Questioning

The biggest shift from the authoritative style of leading to a Transformational Leadership approach occurs when the leader begins to ask questions and is curious, rather than having all the answers. It indicates that you are interested in others' points of view, and that you are willing to gather information before making decisions. Your questions can invite deeper exploration – even transformation.

Begin to pay attention to the quality of your questions – are they **open, forward moving, and curious**? Ask yourself:

- **Is my question "open?" Does it invite further exploration?** *Example: A closed question might be, "Did you enjoy your holiday?" An open and transformational question might be, "What was the most significant experience during your holiday?"*
- **Is my question inviting forward movement toward solutions?** If the question is about the past, the speaker can get stuck in lengthy story-telling and justification. *Example: A "past focused" question might be, "What happened?" A forward focused, transformational question might be, "What did you learn from what happened?"*
- **Is my question based on open curiosity, or am I leading the other person to a conclusion I have already drawn?** Example of a leading question: "Do you agree that the answer is . . .?" Example of a curious question is, "What answers do you have?" A true question is one to which you do not know the answer.

---

**Contemplation:** *How might I use transformational questions to create a more engaging, open environment for others?*

---

# Reflection

*Obstacles I have to asking transformational questions are:*

_____

_____

_____

_____

_____

_____

*Situations I can choose to ask transformational questions that are open, forward moving and curious today would be:*

_____

_____

_____

_____

_____

*Benefits of asking transformational questions in my work situation would be:*

_____

_____

_____

_____

_____

_____

*What I notice after asking transformational questions is:*

_____

_____

_____

_____

_____

_____

# Part 5

---

# A Culture of Transformation

*Step by step, using the Transformational Leadership philosophy, practices, and communication style, the leader begins to create an organizational culture that invites others to grow, learn and transform their lives.*

# Leadership Style of Empowerment

The Transformational Leadership path has two dimensions. One focus is its value for the leader. The leadership role becomes a vehicle for personal growth. The leader is mindful of actions, thoughts, and feelings, and is continuously scanning for clues to increase awareness. He uses the attitude of humility and other disciplines to sharpen his focus, paving the way for transformation.

Another dimension of transformational leadership is about supporting others to grow and transform. It is as if the leader is forging a path or modeling attitudes and behaviors which others may choose to follow.

Leadership that unfolds from the transformational path is that of empowerment. The empowering style of leading focuses on positives and on moving forward, not what has gone wrong or by assigning blame. What do empowering leaders hold as truth? They believe that:

- The employee is their most valuable resource.
- When the employee is encouraged to grow and learn, the organization benefits.
- The leader is in partnership with the employee.
- The leader is a "learner," as well.
- The leader is a listener.
- The employee is fully responsible and accountable.
- The leader makes fair and transparent decisions.
- Integrity and honesty are core values of leaders in the organization.

**Contemplation:** *How might I pay close attention to my style of leadership, which is evident in all my communications, so that I might empower others to transform?*

# Reflection

*I would describe my leadership style as being:*

_____
_____
_____
_____
_____

*The type of leader I would like to become is:*

_____
_____
_____
_____
_____

*Obstacles to becoming this type of leader are:*

_____
_____
_____
_____
_____

*Ways I can move past those obstacles are:*

_____
_____
_____
_____

*A role model for me is:*

_____
_____
_____
_____
_____

# The Culture of Employee Engagement

Employees who are engaged have higher levels of satisfaction and greater productivity. Transformational Leaders not only keep their eye on the "bottom line," but also balance that with taking the temperature of the organization's climate.

What actions support a culture of engagement? Consider these:

- Provide opportunities for the employee to grow – not only professionally, but also personally. Think about professional courses, retreats for personal and professional rejuvenation, and outlets for creative expression within the work environment.
- Provide opportunities for playing and having fun with co-workers.
- Encourage friendships at work.
- Establish regular times for a check-in, not just about performance, but also about personal satisfaction.
- Invite the employee to dream and plan about future opportunities within the organization.
- Support the employee to move out of the organization if growth is leading him/her elsewhere.

Finding ways to show you care about others personally benefits everyone. The rewards are great – both for you, for them, and for the organization. Transformational Leadership naturally allows "employee engagement" to blossom.

---

**Contemplation:** *How might I find ways daily to support employees' personal and professional growth and satisfaction?*

---

# Reflection

*Ways that I already support and engage my employees are:*

_____

_____

_____

_____

_____

_____

_____

*Potential ways to support employee engagement are:*

_____

_____

_____

_____

_____

_____

_____

*Benefits of supporting engagement in my organization would be:*

_____

_____

_____

*Steps I will take today to increase engagement are:*

_____

_____

_____

_____

_____

_____

# Transformational Meetings

Imagine meetings as an opportunity for the leader and others to contribute to a transformational, learning culture. Making sure that your Transformational Leadership approach is evident in meetings is "vital to the vitality" of your organization.

The actualizing leader applies his discipline and philosophy to both one-on-one meetings, and larger group meetings. Some ideas to consider are:

- **Keep your agreement with the timeframe** of the meeting, which demonstrates integrity in terms of respect for self and others.
- **Establish and send the agenda prior to the meeting.** This supports focus, efficiency, and respect.
- **Manage the energy of the meeting.** Require that all communication be respectful. Make sure the conversation is positive and safe, so participants can express their point of view with confidence.
- **Require that all activity within the meeting is focused on the agenda.** Any other activity takes away focus or erodes the respectful nature of the meeting.
- **Intend for the meeting to support a transformational learning culture.** Ask, "What is the learning from our discussion? What values are we supporting? What have we done well, and what can we do better?"
- **Spend time after the meeting reflecting on what you learned.** What is your opportunity for growth?

The leader can use meetings as a vehicle for everyone's benefit. Others will experience the leader using his values in practical ways, and the leader will have an opportunity to learn, grow and transform!

---

**Contemplation:** *How might I design meetings that respect everyone's time and energy, and afford opportunities to learn and grow?*

---

# Reflection

*Obstacles to transformational meetings in my organization are:*

_____

_____

_____

_____

_____

_____

_____

_____

_____

*Steps I will take today to make our meetings reflect a learning, transformational culture are:*

_____

_____

_____

_____

_____

_____

_____

_____

_____

_____

_____

_____

_____

_____

_____

# The "Bottom Line"

Transformational leadership is essentially "inner work." It is a path for personal growth and awareness. It is also about paving a road for others to follow. So, how do productivity and the "bottom-line" fit this inner attitude? Might it be easy to forget the mission of the organization?

The transformational leader must play his role fully, and that includes bottom-line focus. There is a slight shift in emphasis, even though actions and results are similar. Instead of the bottom-line being the ultimate goal, it becomes the litmus test of whether the leader and his organization are aligned with the transformational path.

If the organization's goals are not met, then the transformational leader assesses the situation as a navigator might check his compass. He might ask:

- Is the organization's goal realistic, specific and time appropriate?
- Is the goal in alignment with the organization's values and my personal values?
- What lessons are there for me to learn?
- What obstacles are opportunities for my growth?
- What limiting beliefs or negative attitudes might I or others have that are blocking success?
- What inner adjustments might I make before I correct outer actions?
- How might I have been aware of de-railing clues earlier in the game?

The transformational leader experiences an unmet goal as an opportunity to increase in awareness through reflection and clear action, asking, "What is my learning in relationship to the organization's goal?"

> **Contemplation:** *How might I shift my thinking, so that the organization's goals become a process for learning and greater awareness?*

# Reflection

*A major goal the organization has for me as a leader is:*

_____

_____

_____

_____

_____

*How does this goal relate to my personal values?*

_____

_____

_____

_____

_____

_____

_____

_____

*Attitudes, limiting beliefs or judgments that might be obstacles for me are:*

_____

_____

_____

_____

_____

*New perspective and actions that support my growth as well as the bottom-line are:*

_____

_____

_____

_____

_____

_____

_____

# References and Resources

## Suggested Readings

Belf, Teri-E. *Coaching with Spirit*. San Francisco: Jossey-Bass/Pfeiffer, 2002.

Carson, Richard. *Taming Your Gremlin*. New York: Harper Collins, 2003.

Dyer, Wayne. *Manifest Your Destiny*. New York: Harper Collins, 1999.

Gallwey, Timothy. *The Inner Game of Work*. New York: Random House, 2001.

Goleman, Daniel. *Emotional Intelligence*. New York: Bantam Books, 2006.

Katie, Byron. *Loving What Is*. New York: Three Rivers Press, 2002.

King, Joan C. *The Code of Authentic Living. Cellular Wisdom*. Fort Collins: 2009.

Ladinsky, Daniel. *The Gift: Poems by Hafiz*. New York: Penguin Compass, 1999.

Seligman, Martin. *Learned Optimism*. New York: Pocket Books, 1992.

Singer, Michael A. *The Untethered Soul*. Oakland: New Harbinger Publications, 2007.

Tolle, Eckhart. *The Power of Now*. Novato, CA: New World Library, 1999.

Vitale, Joe. *Zero Limits*. New Jersey: Wiley, 2007

# Recommendations

If you are interested in interviewing someone to be your coach, being trained as a coach, or finding a coaching team for your business or organization, the following professional resources are recommended:

**Vicki Escudé, Executive Leadership Coaching, LLC.**
**www.excellentcoach.com**

Executive Leadership Coaching, LLC and Vicki Escudé, Master Certified Coach, are dedicated to helping you follow your dreams and find ways to move powerfully toward your goals. Coach training is also offered by Vicki Escudé through two ICF Accredited Coach Training Organizations.

**International Coach Federation** (ICF)
**www.coachfederation.org**

The ICF certifies coaches and accredits coaching training schools, and provides ethics, standards of behavior, and coaching competencies for the professional coach.

**Success Unlimited Network®** (SUN)
**www.successunlimitednet.com**

The SUN Coach Training and Certification Program is accredited by the International Coach Federation. SUN is an international coaching and coach training program, supporting coaches to inspire personal and professional growth for individuals who want to learn how to achieve results in all areas of their lives.

**Strategic Executive Coaching Alliance** (SECA)
**www.seca-international.com**

SECA is a global network of coaching leaders, engaging in organizational transformation, certifying qualified professionals and creating extraordinary results through powerful coaching partnerships. The SECA Coach Training and Certification Program is accredited by the International Coach Federation.

# About the Author

**VICKI ESCUDÉ,** M.A., MCC, BCC, Master Coach Trainer, Board Certified Coach, and owner of Executive Leadership Coaching, LLC, is a pioneer in the coaching profession, being the among first to promote the professionalism of coaching to several areas of the United States. She was among the first coach educators for University of Texas-Dallas and Success Unlimited Network (SUN), and is a principal-founder of Strategic Executive Coaching Alliance (SECA). She is co-founder of Advanced Coach Mentoring, providing advanced coach training and mentor certification for coaches who want to deepen their coaching skills.

Her inspiring leadership, group facilitation abilities and joyful, spontaneous style invite a deep exploration of spirit, and encourage expression of one's authentic self. She coaches, trains, supervises and certifies coaches and leaders worldwide, and has been recognized as a successful coach in national publications. Escudé is the author of several books on coaching and leadership. She publishes a monthly newsletter and provides articles for other publications.

Escudé is a graduate of Vanderbilt University, and received her Master's Degree from the University of West Florida in psychology and counseling. She also attended the University of Copenhagen, Denmark. She received additional training with post-graduate work in assessments, facilitation training, and The Byron Katie School of the Work.

Active in the International Coach Federation (ICF) to support the professionalism of coaching, she was elected to the Board of Directors of the ICF for the 2005 to 2008 term. In addition, she has served as an ICF Chapter Founder, on the Ethics Committee, the Membership Committee, and is an Exam Assessor. She volunteers for the Coaching Initiative, in which Master Coaches provide coaching for non-profit CEOs.

www.ingramcontent.com/pod-product-compliance
Lightning Source LLC
Chambersburg PA
CBHW051322170526
45166CB00002B/644